Citizen George
Volume 1

Authored by Michael Dow, RN, MS, MHA, MSM

Drawings by Angel Kincaid

Citizen George
Volume 1

First Edition

ISBN 978-1-968690-08-3

Printed by Lulu.com

Published by Dow Creative Enterprises®

Dow Creative Enterprises, LLC

PO Box 15357

Tucson, AZ 85708

Library of Congress Control Number: 2026907929

Table of Contents

Dedication

The United States of America was blessed with an amazing and outstanding first President, George Washington. He lived an honorable life and respected his fellow citizens. He relinquished power after two terms even though he could have continued in office. He was called the father of his country while he was still living. We are fortunate George Washington wrote a book, and it was about moral living. There are 110 sayings or proverbs that he wanted posterity to consider while pursuing happiness and living a good life. The Citizen George series will be a set of 110 volumes with each volume focusing on one proverb and expounding on it. It is the hope of this writer that the series will help produce future generations of ethical and responsible citizens as George Washington wished.

Michael Dow

Background

Stephen and his uncle George go to the nearby lake to walk around and talk. George likes to take his nephews and nieces on walks to talk about life and living well.

2

“Thank you for spending time with me today Uncle George. I know how busy you are,” says Stephen.

“Family is very important and we should always find time to have high quality experiences with our loved ones,” says George.

"I love coming to this lake. Water is a key to life just like living ethically and responsibly is important for a good life," says George.

“Water lets you do fun things like skipping stones. Living ethically and responsibly lets you do fun things to enjoy life,” says George. George then picks up a stone and slings it across the water, and they watch it skip on top of the water.

“What fun things in life are you talking about?” ask Stephen.

“When you live ethically and responsibly, you can have a good job and have time for good experiences with your family. You can have time to read and travel to new worlds in your mind. You can have time to learn new skills and develop new hobbies that are healthy which increase the quality of your life,” says George.

"When I was raised, I was taught 110 principles to live by to help me live ethically and responsibly. The first rule was 'Every action done in company ought to be done with some sign of respect to those that are present.' The idea of the need to respect others is important and is probably why it was the first rule I was taught," says George.

“How about while we skip stones, we talk about things that are signs of respect that others can observe. We’ll take turns suggesting things,” says George.

“Sounds fun, let’s do it,” says Stephen.

“You go first Stephen,” says George.

“When I talk to someone, I appreciate it when the other person listens carefully to me. How about letting others speak and trying to listen carefully as a sign of respect,” says Stephen.

“Very good. Letting others speak is especially important when the other person is angry," says George.

"Have you ever noticed someone playing with something with their hands or fingers. It seems distracting, like they are not listening to you which we just discussed. Something else that is important is not to fidget in the presence of other people. Fidgeting can be a sign of distraction and inattentiveness," says George.

“I think having good eye contact when you are talking with someone is important. It makes me feel listened to and that the other person has concern for me,” says Stephen.

“You are correct that many cultures view eye contact as a sign of respect. There is a culture that eye contact is not respectful though so that’s why you should learn to know others and what they prefer,” says George.

“This may sound strange but saying things that others wouldn’t dare say and speaking honestly is a sign of respect. Say what you mean, mean what you say, but don’t say it mean,” says George.

“In a way, when people act strangely or erratically, it seems to not care about the other person’s mental well-being, so I think having control over your emotions is important to be respectful to those around you,” says Stephen.

“You’re correct. You also want to learn to have a straight face with no emotion even though something may be said or done that could cause a person to show extreme shock,” says George.

“Being focused especially on what is being said and what the other person is trying to convey is very important. Focused attention is important because we live in a complicated world and not everything is simple. This goes back to what we started with which was listen to others carefully,” says George.

“I think growing means you must learn who you are meant to be as a person. Being true to yourself is respecting life and being thankful for the life that has been given to us,” says Stephen.

“Well said. Know yourself and then be true to who you know yourself to be,” says George.

"Mindfulness is also a key to respecting life. You want to be mindful of the moment you are in, so you are fully present with your family, friends, acquaintances, and strangers. People need you and your attention is something free that you can give them to show you care and respect them," says George.

"I've always like it when someone says things to me to show they are listening. That seems important," says Stephen.

"I agree, active listening is important. If you are actively listening and saying occasional words to show you are listening, it is usually always appreciated by the other person. Paying attention to them helps show you are not wasting their time," says George.

"In my opinion, dressing sharply is a sign that you respect the other person. It is not just a sign of respect for yourself, but it also shows that you are wanting to help the other person express good feelings to you. Sometimes, making it easy for others to be kind to you can also be seen as respect," says George.

“I think speaking purposefully is respectful. Having meaning and purpose in your speech shows you are respecting the time that the other person is giving you,” says Stephen.

“Not wasting the other person’s time is important since it is one of the few resources you never get back,” says George.

“Avoiding to simply please everyone all the time is not something you want to start doing since people will doubt your intentions. Again, be true to yourself while respecting others,” says George.

“I think giving to others and being generous is respectful because it shows you have concern for the other person’s needs and wants. Helping someone with material things shows care for their life,” says Stephen.

“Yes, it is. Great point,” says George.

"Also, if you appreciate someone for what they have said or done to help you, it is important that you tell them that you appreciate them instead of only thinking it. Words and compliments are free so we should freely thank people for their time and efforts," says George.

“I really enjoyed spending time and talking with you Uncle George. Thanks for taking time to spend with me and helping me feel special,” says Stephen.

“You’re welcome,” says George as they start to skip stones again.

George and Stephen then leave the lake and walk back to the house. Stephen thinks about what was said throughout the day and practices these ideas with his mom and dad.

References

Mothers, A. (2024). 14 Signs a Person Is Genuinely Respected, According to Psychology. Retrieved from: https://www.yourtango.com/self/signs-person-genuinely-respected

Journal

What page number was your favorite drawing?

What were three things you learned?

Do you have any new questions about life from reading this book?

What do you plan to do differently in your life after reading this book?

About the Illustrator

Angel Kincaid is an artist who studied at, Art Instruction School, American National, and the University of Kentucky for various kinds of art. She is a forensic artist and is also trained in illustration as well as classical painting. She lives in Lexington, Kentucky with her husband and lil' dog. Originally from Utah, she found she loved art at a young age and has studied and done art her whole life. She is currently working on her PhD in forensics/forensic art at the University of Kentucky and looking forward to doing more with her art career.

About the Author

Michael is married to Perla, and they have three children. Michael served in the US Air Force between 2002 and 2010 as an Electronic Warfare Officer on the EC-130H Compass Call and deployed 6 times in the Global War on Terror. Michael then served 8 years as an Army Wounded Warrior Advocate. Michael used his GI bill to go to nursing school and works as an RN at an inpatient psychiatric hospital in Tucson, AZ. Michael enjoys listening to Beethoven and reading a lot of news.

Michael's college education:

B.A. in Psychology from Auburn University,

B.S. in Biology from the University of Alabama at Birmingham,

M.S. in Management from Troy University,

Master in Health Administration from the University of Phoenix,

M.S. from the University of Arizona through the accelerated Master's Entry to the Profession of Nursing program

Other Books by Dow Creative Enterprises®

Nurse Florence®

www.nurseflorence.org

Nurse Dorothea®

www.nursedorothea.com

Citizen George

www.citizengeorge.com

Nurse Clara

www.NurseClara.org

Visit www.DowCreativeEnterprises.com for more information

www.ingramcontent.com/pod-product-compliance
Lightning Source LLC
LaVergne TN
LVHW020626110826
845149LV00004B/1050

9781968690083